ruach 5771 songbook

includes CD (also available separately)

Editors
Michael Boxer
Jayson Rodovsky

Typesetter
Joshua Wiczer

TRANSCONTINENTAL
MUSIC Publications
The world's leading publisher of Jewish music since 1938

Visit **www.RuachCD.com**
for artist information, educational material, and downloads

RUACH 5771 SONGBOOK: NEW JEWISH TUNES

© 2011 Transcontinental Music Publications
A division of URJ Books and Music
633 Third Avenue - New York, NY 10017 - Fax 212.650.4119
212.650.4105 - **www.TranscontinentalMusic.com** - tmp@urj.org
993432

Manufactured in the United States of America
Cover design by Roy Clark, Pine Point Productions - Windham, ME
Book design by Joel N. Eglash
Additional design by Michael Boxer
ISBN 8074-1177-3
10 9 8 7 6 5 4 3 2 1

PREFACE

RUACH IS THE HEBREW WORD FOR *SPIRIT*. It is exactly *that* quality which the songs of the *Ruach* series possess. These songs were chosen for their ear-catching melodies, their colorful instrumental support, and for the life the music breathes into their texts. In short, all this is summed up by one common trait: *ruach*.

The *Ruach* series is the continuation of the seven original NFTY (North American Federation of Temple Youth) albums that were recorded between 1972 and 1989 (see the NFTY five-CD set available from Transcontinental Music). The NFTY and *Ruach* albums are primary sources of participatory music for cantors, songleaders, musical leaders and all those who disseminate Jewish music. Through their leadership, the tradition of singing is passed on to the next generation of campers and youth groupers: the future songleaders, cantors, and musical leaders. This songbook is another way of preserving this musical tradition for future generations.

Joel N. Eglash
Series Creator

Thanks are due to Cantor Rosalie Boxt, Adrian Durlester, Steve Fontaine, Rabbi Dan Freelander, Eric Komar, Jonathan Levine, Rabbi Michael Mellen, Victor Ney, Rachel Wetstein; the members of the *Ruach 5771* committee, whose varying backgrounds and experiences helped shape this remarkable collection of music; and, of course, the artists who have created this great music for all of us.

RUACH 5771 COMMITTEE

Michael Boxer
Steve Brodsky
Michael Goldberg
Cantor Alane Katzew
Jesse Paikin
Jayson Rodovsky
Caryn Roman
Sean Thibault

FOREWORD

Music, so powerfully, has become the language of those who pursue justice. The songs we sing have a way of becoming anthems – think "We Shall Overcome," think "Let My People Go," think "Oseh Shalom Bimromav." This disc brings together some of the most creative names, both established and emerging stars, in some of the most inspiring tracks, popular and new, in Jewish music. It amplifies the message that echoes through 50 years of the social justice work we have all pursued with the Religious Action Center since 1961.

The songs on this CD represent the contemporary soundtrack of our Movement: our camps, our congregations, and our families; our social action work, our worship, our communal gatherings. They may be remembered in the future as the anthems of this generation's vital civil rights and social justice struggles. And you, dear listener, will be remembered as the *tikkun olam* activists that helped bring about a more just world.

Enjoy! And pursue!

Rabbi David Saperstein
Director, Religious Action Center of Reform Judaism

Hebrew Pronunciation Guide

VOWELS
a as in *father*
ai as in *aisle* (= long *i* as in *ice*)
e = short *e* as in *bed*
ei as in *eight* (= long *a* as in *ace*)
i as in *pizza* (= long *e* as in *be*)
o = long *o* as in *go*
u = long *u* as in *lunar*
' = unstressed vowel close to ə or unstressed short *e*

CONSONANTS
ch as in German *Bach* or Scottish *loch* (not as in *cheese*)
g = hard *g* as in **get** (not soft *g* as in **gem**)
tz = as in *boats*
h after a vowel is silent

ruach 5771

ruach 5771 songbook

oseh shalom by elana jagoda

may the one who makes peace

text: liturgy
music: elana jagoda

> *Oseh Shalom* is often sung as the culminating prayer for worship services as it comes from the concluding line of the *Kaddish*, the *Amidah* and *Birkat HaMazon*. We ask that we may know peace in our land, peace in our hearts and peace for all people. There is great power in collective prayer and song. My hope is that this melody inspires you to sing boldly. I believe our voices can and will bring peace down.

May the One who makes peace in the high heavens
make peace for us.

עֲשֶׂה שָׁלוֹם בִּמְרוֹמָיו,
הוּ יַעֲשֶׂה שָׁלוֹם עָלֵינוּ.

Copyright © 2010 Elana Jagoda

993432

sweet as honey
by dan nichols and e18hteen

la'asok b'divrei torah

hebrew text: liturgy
english text and music: dan nichols

> When young students are introduced to Torah study, it is often with a drop of honey on their finger, so that the words of Torah might be sweet to them. As it is written, "*B'fichah U'vilvavcha La'asoto* -- the thing (Torah) is very close to you, in your mouth, and in your heart to observe it" (Deut. 30:14). Dan Nichols' song *Sweet as Honey* brings the words of blessing that precede Torah study together with a prompt to be mindful that our study always be a sweet experience.
>
> -- Cantor Alane Katzew

993432

Blessed are You, Adonai our God,
Sovereign of the universe,
who hallows us with mitzvot,
commanding us to engage with words of Torah.

בָּרוּךְ אַתָּה, יְיָ
אֱלֹהֵינוּ, מֶלֶךְ הָעוֹלָם,
אֲשֶׁר קִדְּשָׁנוּ בְּמִצְוֹתָיו
וְצִוָּנוּ לַעֲסוֹק בְּדִבְרֵי תוֹרָה.

993432

jerusalem by michelle citrin

text & music: michelle citrin

During the 2nd Israel-Lebanon conflict, I was sitting in a cafe overlooking the Old City of Jerusalem noticing how divided the city was like pieces of a puzzle. I realized that since the beginning of its existence, everyone wanted to claim this beautiful city as their own. This is a city that is constantly being fought over! Just then, I noticed reporters roaming the streets, helicopters above, and the news channels reporting what peoples' response to the conflict was in Jerusalem. Once again, the whole world has their eye on Jerusalem, the city of peace gone to pieces.

993432

8

reach our hands out by soulaviv

text & music: robert raede

ruach 57 71 track 4

> *Reach Our Hands Out* is a classic *'tikkun olam'* song. It's about looking around us, finding people who are less fortunate, and finding ways to help them and make the world a little better and brighter. Sometime in our lives we all need the kindness of strangers. This song seems to really reach our audiences, and it affects us too -- it makes Roxanne, who sings it live, cry sometimes when she introduces it. Hope you like it.

Funk (♩= 110)

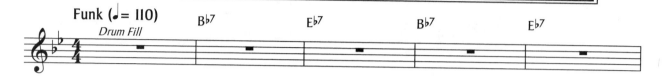
Drum Fill

1. I look a-round I see peo-ple down and cry-ing for com-pass - ion___

I hear the sound of lots of talk but no one's tak-ing ac - tion.___

There's more that I___ can do. There's more that I___ can be. And if you feel___ it too

Won't you walk___ with me? And reach our hands out___

(make a bet-ter place)___ reach our hands out___ (make a bright-er place)___

reach our hands out___ It's on-ly by___ the grace of God and fate that

993432

993432

make it a bridge by steve meltzer

kol ha'olam kulo

english text: sheldon young
music: steve meltzer
hebrew lyrics: reb nachman of bratzlav

"My husband Steve Meltzer, a beloved teacher, youth group advisor, songleader, and composer, died unexpectedly on April 7, 2009 at the age of 45. 'Make it a Bridge' was one of his last recordings, written in memory of the late Lenny Zakim (z"l), a respected civil rights leader in Boston who died in 1999 after a 5-year battle with cancer. A new bridge over the Charles River in Boston was named in his memory, and when the bridge was dedicated, a poem written by Sheldon Young called "Make it a Bridge" was published in The Jewish Advocate. Steve set these beautiful words to music and recorded the song in October of 2008, but it was not heard publicly until our friends in the band Sababa performed it at a memorial concert for Steve a few days after he died. It became the title song of 'Make It a Bridge: Remembering Steve Meltzer,' a memorial CD featuring seven of Steve's original songs and eight others contributed by his friends, colleagues and mentors. In tribute to Steve, proceeds from the sale of this recording fund scholarships for aspiring song leaders to attend *Hava Nashira*, an annual event that Steve loved so much."

– Beth Meltzer

993432

14

16

when we reach each o-ther's side the walls in-be-tween will
dis - ap - pear. 3. There is a wall
stand - ing be - tween us, a
wall so wide it seems not to end.
But if we em-brace as bro-thers and sis -
- ters we can breach the wall
and make it a bridge. Kol ha - o - lam
ku - lo ge - sher tzar m' - od

The entire world is but a narrow bridge;
the most important thing is not to be afraid.

כָּל הָעוֹלָם כֻּלּוֹ גֶּשֶׁר צַר מְאֹד
וְהָעִקָּר לֹא לְפַחֵד כְּלָל.

daniel's round by the levins

hebrew text: daniel 12:3
music & english text: ira and julia levin

ruach 57 71 track 6

> Daniel's Round was inspired by Daniel 12:3: "The enlightened will shine like the zohar of the sky, and those who make the masses righteous will shine like the stars forever and ever". What inspired us about this text was the act of turning many to righteousness- not seeking power or self glorification but a universal *Teshuva* that brings us back to being connected to each other and to the Source of our well being.

Instrumental Introduction

♩ = 72

Chorus

Those that turn turn turn ma-ny___ to right-eous - ness Will

shine shine shine with hea-ven's sweet_____ car - ess.

1. And those that can dis-cern___ will shine with bless-ings from on high Like the

dome of hea-ven's fir - ma-ment Like a Zo-har in the sky.___

993432

2. V'-ha-ma-ski-lim yaz-hi-ru k'-zo-har ha-ra-ki-yah u-matz-di-kei ha-ra-bim ka ko-cha-vim l'-o-lam va-ed.

Those that turn turn turn ma-ny to right-eous-ness Will

And those that can dis-cern will shine with bless-ings from on high Like the

shine shine shine with hea-ven's sweet car-ess. And

dome of hea-ven's fir-ma-ment Like a Zo-har in the sky. V'-ha-

those that can dis-cern will shine with bless-ings from on high Like the

ma-ski-lim yaz-hi-ru k'-zo-har ha-ra-ki-yah u-

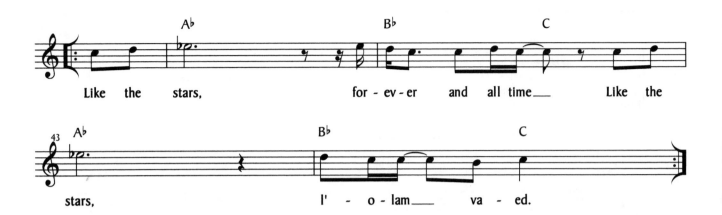

Like the stars, for - ev - er and all time___ Like the

stars, l' - o - lam___ va - ed.

The enlightened will shine like the zohar of the sky,
and those who make the masses righteous
will shine like the stars forever and ever.

וְהַמַּשְׂכִּלִים יַזְהִרוּ כְּזֹהַר הָרָקִיעַ
וּמַצְדִּיקֵי הָרַבִּים כַּכּוֹכָבִים לְעוֹלָם וָעֶד.

it could be amazing by jay rapoport

text & music: jay rapoport

In December 2009, I was in Jerusalem leading a group of American and Israeli teens on a UJA-Federation Partnership 2000 exchange program. We visited Yad B'Yad, a school where Jews and Arabs learn together (www.handinhandk12.org), and as we heard from the school's leaders about their vision of a more peaceful future for Israel, I was inspired to write the words of this song. I was thrilled to perform it for the first time when the Israeli teens visited us in New York in April 2010 at Congregation Rodeph Sholom!

1. His - to - ry could teach us a - ny - thing___ We
look to our past___ and see where we're go - ing___ But his - to - ry won't tell us
ev - ery-thing___ And some of those___ things___ are real-ly worth___ know - ing___
If___ we say it's not a-bout___ us___ It's a - bout the next___ gen - er -
a - tion___ Take a look at the fu - ture___ we are
fac - ing.___ Some peo-ple say we are hope - less___

993432

Some peo-ple say we are cra - zy___ But if we be - lieve___ in a

bet - ter dream___ Hal - le - lu - jah___ it could be a -

maz - ing___

2. Fam - i - ly is where we start - ed___ To know your - self___ you need to

know where you come___ from___ E - ven-tu-ally you choose your own___ path___ Un -

stea-dy at___ first,___ now look what you've be-come___ If___ I say it's

not a-bout___ me___ It's a - bout the next___ ge - ner - a - tion___

Take a look at the fu - ture___ I am mak - ing___ oh___

24

993432

hineini by peri smilow

i am here

text: adapted from the text of the seven kavanot for mikveh preparation, created by mayyim hayyim living waters community mikveh
music: peri smilow

Until recently the notion of mikveh had no connection to my every day life. It was simply a ritual bath for traditional Jews. I had no idea that visiting one could help a cancer patient return to life or help a 75 year old woman celebrate her birthday or provide comfort to someone facing the dissolution of a marriage. Then friends of mine dreamed of a beautiful pool where all Jews could reclaim the beauty of this ancient tradition. And it was so. This song was commissioned by Mayyim Hayyim Living Waters Community Mikveh in Newton, MA. The blessings sung in this piece are recited by those who enter the healing waters of the mikveh.

993432

Here I am.
I am made in the image of God.
You fashioned the human being intricate in design.
The soul in me is pure.

הִנֵּנִי.
בְּצֶלֶם אֱלֹהִים.
נְקָבִים נְקָבִים.
נִשְׁמָתִי טְהוֹרָה הִיא.

sim shalom by mikey pauker

grant us peace

text: liturgy - amidah
music: mikey pauker

ruach
57 • 71
track 9

> During my first summer as a song-leader at URJ Camp Newman, I remember sitting in the song-leading office jamming with a few members of my team. We were discussing about our favorite contemporary Jewish artists and what makes a Jewish melody a "hit." Following our conversation, I decided to give writing a Jewish song a try and started singing this melody of *Sim Shalom*. Both Leah Shafritz and Shoshana Jarvis joined me on harmonies and an hour later I finished writing my first Jewish song. After teaching this melody and singing it during our services, I knew we had created something magical. It was a pleasure to lay down this track with my engineer and producer Troy Dexter. I mentioned that I wanted the song to be orchestrated with a full band including a cello. Troy created a stellar string arrangement, and turned my dream of cellos into a reality. Troy also brought Julie Silver and Leah Shafritz into the studio to record the three part harmony. This song still resonates with my soul every time I sing it. I hope you enjoy. B'shalom.

993432

993432

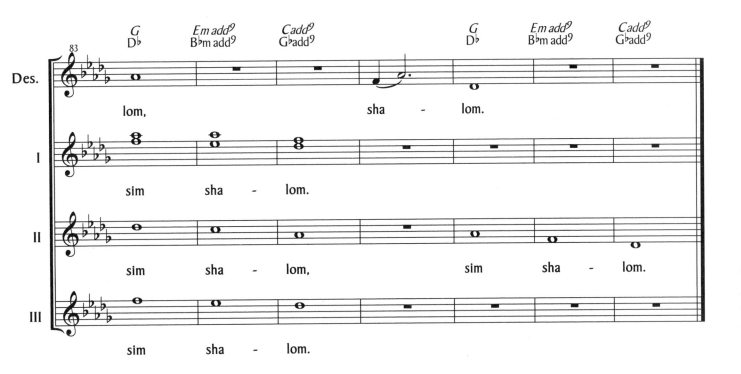

Grant peace, goodness and blessing,
grace, kindness and mercy,
to us and to all Your people Israel.

שִׂים שָׁלוֹם טוֹבָה וּבְרָכָה,
חֵן וָחֶסֶד וְרַחֲמִים,
עָלֵינוּ וְעַל כָּל יִשְׂרָאֵל עַמֶּךָ.

salaam achshav *by* jeremy gimbel and shira tirdof

peace, now

text & music: jeremy gimbel
& bradley lennox

> Musically, "Salaam Achshav" is an homage to the Dave Matthews Band song, "Grey Street," a favorite of mine. Lyrically, I really tried to get the point across that rallies and lectures about peace are necessary and wonderful, but at some point our leaders actually have to do something about it. The song came out of a place of frustration. For years, we have seen these movements to make something happen and to create a lasting peace, but we're still left in conflict. While conflict in general is inevitable, in present day Israel, it has gone on long enough. There must be some way to make a successful and lasting peace. And while I am not nearly qualified enough to be at the negotiation tables, this song is a call to action for those who can realize that the time for action is now.

993432

993432

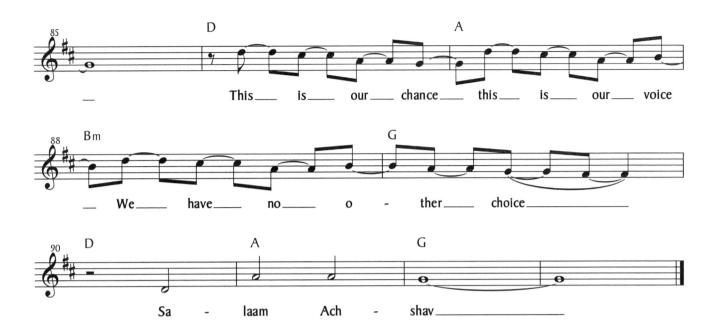

Peace, now!

שָׁלַאם אַחְשָׁב

adonai s'fatai tiftach by cantor natalie young

adonai, open my lips

text: amidah
music: natalie young

I remember sitting out on the mirpeset (balcony) of my Jerusalem apartment my first year of cantorial school. Guitar in hand, my fingers discovered this beautiful chord progression. From somewhere deep within came a haunting melody to the meditative words of *Adonai S'fatai*. The two harmonies that are woven in, first emerged as their own melodic lines. I was blessed by talented friends and colleagues who gave life to this song for the first time that year in Israel. The band of Milk and Honey, made up of some of my closest friends, nurtured my song-writing throughout my years at HUC, and through their kind generosity, have finally enabled me to record this song the way it was meant to be. The talented Beth Schafer helped create this beautiful arrangement.

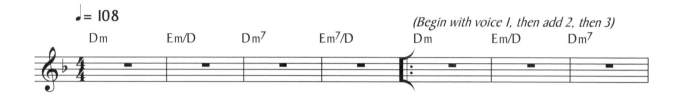

993432

Adonai, open up my lips,
that my mouth may declare Your praise.

אֲדֹנָי, שְׂפָתַי תִּפְתָּח,
וּפִי יַגִּיד תְּהִלָּתֶךָ.

993432

the call by ross m. levy

text & music: ross m. levy

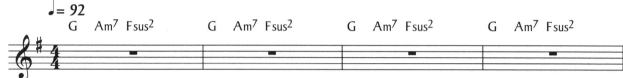

After the devastating earthquake in Haiti in 2010 I felt compelled to do something more than write a check. We often forget about these disasters when the headlines stop. It can be "trendy" to get involved with a cause for a week or two and then forget all about it. This song is a constant reminder to us all that each day is the opportune time to get involved and make a difference. I hope "*The Call*" will become a mantra for social action activism in the future.

993432

mi chamochah by josh nelson

who is like you

text: evening shabbat liturgy
music: josh nelson

Right now, it's hard to just 'be.' These are complicated, uncertain times... Unsure, we have paused at the threshold of this doorway, scared to step forward into something bigger than ourselves. Like the Israelites at the shores of the sea, may we be brave enough to step into the water... so that we might emerge on the other side, stronger and more whole. *Adonai yimloch l'olam vaed;* And God shall reign for ever and ever. Let this be our blessing.

993432

Who is like You, O god, among the gods that are worshipped!
Who is like You, majestic in holiness,
awesome in splendor, working wonders!

Your children witnessed Your sovereignty,
the sea splitting before Moses and Miriam.
"This is our God!" they cried.
"Adonai will reign forever and ever!"

מִי־כָמֹכָה בָּאֵלִם, יְיָ!
מִי כָּמֹכָה נֶאְדָּר בַּקֹּדֶשׁ,
נוֹרָא תְהִלֹּת, עֹשֵׂה פֶלֶא!

מַלְכוּתְךָ רָאוּ בָנֶיךָ,
בּוֹקֵעַ יָם לִפְנֵי מֹשֶׁה וּמִרְיָם.
זֶה אֵלִי, עָנוּ וְאָמְרוּ,
יְיָ יִמְלֹךְ לְעֹלָם וָעֶד!

esah einai *by* alan goodis

i lift my eyes

english text & music: alan goodis
hebrew text: psalm 121:1-2

> *Esah Einai* was written in 2008 after the unexpected death of my wife's family friend. Death is always sad and difficult for anyone mourning a loss. Yet, we can often find comfort and peace in knowing a person lived a full life and is no longer ill of body, mind or spirit. When a young person dies it is more difficult to feel that sense of comfort. In sitting down to wrap my brain around what had happened and write this song, I stumbled upon the words to Psalm 121: 1-2—I lift my eyes to the mountains; from where does my help come? My help comes from God, maker of heaven and earth. I had this image of a literal mountain of grief, pain and doubt that stood before all those who were mourning this death. I felt this mountain was a test of one's faith and belief that God would ultimately prove to be our help and allow us to find peace. The lyrics of the song are meant to capture the journey of the climb towards the summit of the mountain. On this journey all those who are mourning are uttering the words, *Esah einai el heharim, mei-ayim yavo, yavo ezri?*, as a mantra with the hope that if these words are repeated enough we will find what are looking for: rest, sleep, peace, comfort and strength.

993432

48

I lift my eyes to the mountains; from where does my help come?

אֶשָּׂא עֵינַי אֶל־הֶהָרִים, מֵאַיִן יָבֹא עֶזְרִי?

war no more by jon nelson & yom hadash

lo yisa goi

text: jon nelson, based on isaiah 2:4
music: jon nelson

> Writing and producing "War No More" was really a labor of love. I have always loved the different melodies to "Lo Yisa Goi" and the notion of "laying down swords in favor of peace." It's an idea that's been around for many years, being really prevalent in the folk genre. I wanted to find a way to take those universal feelings, and fuse them with straight ahead rock & roll... complete with the urgency and energy of the classic rock that I grew up with. I first wrote the riff, and the rest of the song seemed to fall into place. When I perform this song live with my band, Yom Hadash, it always gets a great response from all ages. My band mates really brought the arrangement to life and it's one of my personal favorites. Enjoy!

993432

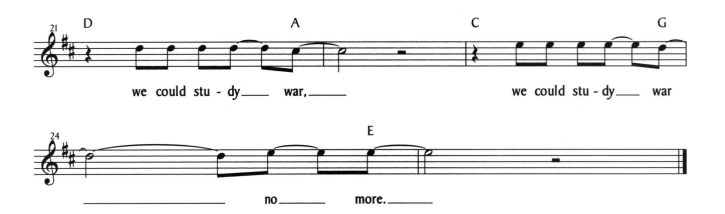

we could stu - dy___ war,___ we could stu - dy___ war

___ no___ more.___

Nation shall not take up sword against nation;
they shall never again study war.

לֹא־יִשָּׂא גוֹי אֶל־גּוֹי חֶרֶב,
לֹא־יִלְמְדוּ עוֹד מִלְחָמָה.

hoshiah *by* dan nichols and e18hteen

god delivers

text: psalm 28:9
music: dan nichols

> "*Hoshia et amecha...* Help Your people. Bless Your heritage. Tend them and exalt them forever." Set by Dan Nichols is this fresh contemporary setting of the ancient text from Psalm 28:9. From the moment it was first introduced to those gathered at Hava Nashira (songleading institute) in 2007 and then at URJ camps across the country, Hoshia has spread like wildfire. Its driving rhythmic intensity made it an overnight sensation and a "must-include" during song sessions across the Reform landscape.
>
> -- Cantor Alane Katzew

Start slowly and speed up (1st Time: ♩= 84, 2nd Time: ♩ = 100, 3rd Time: ♩ = 108)

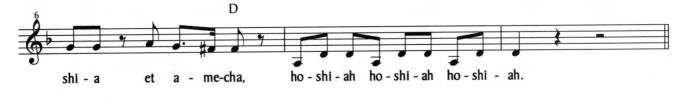

993432

54

Save Your people; bless Your heritage.
Tend them and exalt them forever.

הוֹשִׁיעָה אֶת עַמֶּךָ וּבָרֵךְ אֶת נַחֲלָתֶךָ
וּרְעֵם וְנַשְּׂאֵם עַד הָעוֹלָם.

rise up by craig taubman

text & music: craig taubman

ruach 57 71 track 17

> How many *Shema*'s are left to be written? How many songs can we listen to? This is my 4th or 5th interpretation of this text. Each song comes from a different place and time in my life. Some are uplifting (*Master Of All Things*) and others were instructive (*V'shinantam/Talmud Torah k'neged kulam*). *Rise Up* comes against the backdrop of experiences I have had in interfaith circles. Every faith practice demands you to love your God. Rise up...raise your voices, love your God.

Rock with 16th feel (♩= 116)

Love your God With all your heart With all your might With all your soul Love your God With all your heart With all your mind With all your soul Where you stand Where you lie When you walk And when you rise Rise up Raise your voic-es Rise up lift them high Rise up we can raise our voic-es Rise up

993432

let it be me by rick recht

elohai n'tzor

text & music : rick recht

Rick Recht's 'Let it Be Me' is found on his Tear Down the Walls album (www.rickrecht.com/music), a collection of songs focused on celebration of diversity. The lyrics of Let it Be Me include the phrase, 'Elohai, N'tzor ' which is found in the Amidah, translated: "Guard my tongue from evil and my mouth from speaking falsehoods." Let it Be Me is song about self-empowerment. Let it Be Me is about individuals recognizing the opportunities we all have to make a difference in this world. Let it Be Me, Recht focuses on the power of words to have exponential positive impact in the world. Words can love, protect, and comfort. The chorus includes the words, Elohai N'tzor – a call to avoid gossip and the ability words have to negatively impact the world.

993432

60

993432

My God, guard my speech from evil
and my lips from deception.

אֱלֹהַי, נְצֹר לְשׁוֹנִי
מֵרָע וּשְׂפָתַי מִדַּבֵּר מִרְמָה.

eliyahu hanavi by max chaiken

elijah the prophet

text & music: max chaiken

This song came to me late one summer afternoon in 2006 while I was thinking about the profound difference between what I was taught that we, as Reform Jews, are praying for when we sing *Eliyahu Hanavi*, and what many other Jews hope or pray for when singing this beautiful, traditional text. That we must engage in actively repairing the world was my focus, and I hope that this setting for *Eliyahu Hanavi* helps to convey that.

E - li -ya - hu ha - na - vi, E - li -ya - hu ha - tish - bi,

E - li -ya - hu ha - na - vi, E-li-ya - hu__ ha - gi - la - di. Bim-hei-rah__ b' - ya-mei-nu,

ya - vo__ ei - lei - nu, im Ma-shi - ach ben Da-vid, im Ma-shi - ach ben Da-vid.__

1. We are wait-ing for__ a time to come when in-jus - tice shall be gone

Pain and vio - lence will be no more done with ha - tred done with war And

all the peo - ple in the land will lend their voi - ces lend their hand

That day starts with you and__ me and E - li -ya - hu Ha - na - vi.

993432

May Elijah the prophet, Elijah the Tishbite,
Elijah of Gilead,
quickly in our day come to us
heralding redemption.

אֵלִיָּהוּ הַנָּבִיא, אֵלִיָּהוּ הַתִּשְׁבִּי,
אֵלִיָּהוּ הַגִּלְעָדִי,
בִּמְהֵרָה בְיָמֵינוּ, יָבוֹא אֵלֵינוּ,
עִם מָשִׁיחַ בֶּן־דָּוִד.

artist biographies

MAX CHAIKEN is a professional Jewish musician, educator and song leader. After graduating from Brown University in 2009, he moved north to the Boston area to pursue Jewish music and education full time. He currently teaches at Temple Beth Shalom in Needham, MA, as well as at The Rashi School (Dedham) and MetroWest Jewish Day School (Framingham). He served as a song leader for NFTY Convention in 2009 in Washington, D.C., and also served as the head song leader for URJ Camp Harlam from 2004 through 2009. Max has worked with many synagogues, college Hillels, and youth groups throughout New England and around the country, and is very excited and honored to be a part of Ruach 5771.

MICHELLE CITRIN is a Brooklyn-based singer/songwriter and composer, best known to Jewish communities around the world as the star of YouTube sensations "20 Things to do with Matzah" and "Rosh Hashanah Girl." Michelle tours internationally, appearing at festivals, clubs, universities and JCCs. Recent performances include the URJ Biennial, Limmud UK, NY and LA, as well as at the 40th anniversary of Tel Aviv's Birthright Mega Event. Michelle's engaging soulful stage presence, insightful lyrics and memorable hooks have garnered rave reviews and accolades, including being named as one of Billboard Music's Top Songwriters and as a finalist for VH-1's Song of the Year. The New York *Jewish Week* included Michelle in its list of "36 Under 36: The Next Wave of Jewish Innovators." Currently, Michelle is scoring the music and lyrics for the upcoming Broadway production of *Sleepless in Seattle*, and is set to launch her debut full length album, *Left Brained, Right Hearted*.

JEREMY GIMBEL was the Youth Director at Congregation Beth Israel in San Diego from 2008-2011. Previously, he served as head song leader at URJ Camp Newman in Santa Rosa, CA and as song leader for various synagogue functions and NFTY events throughout California. His band, **SHIRA TIRDOF**, released their debut album, *A Blessing In Disguise,* in 2005, showcasing their Jewish rock style with distinct Jewish camp influences, and their most recent album, *Let It Happen*, has received great reviews. Jeremy is most proud of his work as editor of *Birkon Mikdash M'at*, the Reform movement's first bencher, and his accomplishments while serving as NFTY's Religious and Cultural Vice President. Jeremy formed his Jewish identity as a camper at URJ Camp Newman/Swig and Kutz, through his involvement in NFTY, and growing up in his native San Diego, CA. Jeremy is married to Sarah Gimbel.

ALAN GOODIS is a national touring Jewish musician. Born and raised in Toronto, Canada, Alan is a proud product of URJ Goldman Union Camp Institute. Noted for his dedication to building relationships and community through music, Alan travels the country to serve as an artist-in-residence and performer at synagogues, Hillels, youth conventions, and Jewish summer camps. His 2009 self-titled debut CD, produced by and performed with Dan Nichols (e18hteen) and Grammy-nominee Mark Niemiec, elevates Jewish music with its powerful vocals and bold melodies. Alan is a strong presence in the Reform Jewish movement and works tirelessly to engage, educate and empower Jewish youth and adults through music. Alan lives in Chicago, IL with his wife Codi.

ELANA JAGODA is a performer, composer, prayer leader and educator who brings soul and innovation to Jewish music. She adds new dimensions to this music genre by blending her energetic folk-rock vibe with her passion for world music. Elana infuses a unique spiritual quality into the music she brings to both performance and prayer. Elana released her first solo album, *Zum Gali Gali*, in 2007. She revamped classic Jewish family songs with a funky-modern flavor. Her new CD, *Uri Uri*, is a creative fusion of musical styles that elegantly speaks to both kids and adults alike. Both CDs have been selected for national distribution through the PJ Library program. Elana plays rocking family concerts with her band at synagogues, museums, festivals and community centers. She currently serves as the full-time cantorial soloist at Peninsula Temple Beth El in San Mateo, California.

THE LEVINS' music celebrates Tanach, the Talmud and the Sufi poetry of Hafiz with a lyrical mysticism that inspires joy! They have been featured at the Jewish Music Festival in Amsterdam, Limmud in Coventry, England, Shalshelet in New York City and across America. Their concerts are filled with songs and stories that accentuate the connection between communities, with a light-hearted depth that delights Jewish audiences and reaches beyond borders.

ROSS M. LEVY has been a force on the Jewish music scene, playing for congregations, camps, and youth groups around the country. He has received accolades from congregations up and down the East coast for his original style of music, which combines a unique sound with witty lyrics that keeps audiences captivated and coming back for more. Ross has performed hundreds of shows, including performances at NFTY National Convention, URJ Regional Biennial Conventions, and CAJE Conferences. Ross was even crowned the winner of the Rising Star competition at CAJE 34 in Vermont. He has released two albums of original Jewish music, and has been previously featured on *Ruach 5767* and *Ruach 5769*. Ross has also been a featured artist on OySongs, and can be heard daily on Jewish Rock Radio. When asked about what kind of music he makes, he smiles and simply says, "Jewish music that cooks!" Ross lives in Philadelphia with his wife, Cantor Amy E. Levy and his two beautiful daughters, Aria and Kira.

On April 7, 2009, the contemporary Jewish music community was shocked and saddened by the sudden death of **STEVE MELTZER**, a talented musician and dear friend to many, at the age of 45. Steve had been singing and songleading for 20 years. Born in New York City and raised in Long Island, NY, Steve was very active in his home congregation, Temple Emanuel in Lynbrook, NY. A product of the Eisner and Kutz camps, Steve's songleading and performing had been influenced by Steve Dropkin (his counselor at Eisner in 1977), Cantor Jeff Klepper, and Debbie Friedman. A graduate of Tulane University (where he double-majored in English and Jewish Studies), Steve pursued a Master's in Jewish Education (MJEd) and a Cantorial Arts Certificate at Hebrew College in Newton, MA. Steve led songs at five URJ camps, performed at numerous other camps and synagogues from New York to Louisiana, and taught, directed youth groups and performed as a cantorial soloist at synagogues in the Boston area. Steve's first CD, *Rock With Ruach*, was released in 2008, and he had been preparing to release a new CD of his original songs but was unable to finish the work. His devoted parents and wife of 18 years, Beth, decided to complete the project in his memory, and through tireless effort with the help of Steve's peers, friends and mentors, including many of the well-known contemporary Jewish music artists with whom Steve had shared the stage, completed *Make It A Bridge: Remembering Steve Meltzer* in 2010. Steve's legacy of dedication to Jewish music lives on as sales of that album support the Make It a Bridge Fund, which helps aspiring song leaders attend Hava Nashira, the URJ's annual music and song leading workshop, an event that Steve loved dearly.

For over a decade, **JON NELSON** has been a mainstay in modern Jewish music. As the founder of the groundbreaking Jewish rock band **YOM HADASH**, he's performed hundreds of concerts from coast to coast. Having released six full-length CDs, his original songs and liturgical settings have become part of the fabric of many synagogues across the United States. Composing music that cross genres and boundaries, his songs can be heard heard on radio rotations in the United States, Canada, Israel and beyond. A native of New Bedford, MA, Jon graduated from the University of Massachusetts at Amherst and holds a Master's degree in

Education. He currently resides in Rhode Island with his wife Beth and their children, Ben, Evan and Emily. In addition to touring with Yom Hadash and Jon Nelson's Rockin' Kids Revue (his rock band especially geared towards young children), Jon is also a cantorial soloist and educator in the greater Boston area.

JOSH NELSON is one of the most popular performers and producers in modern Jewish music. A multi-instrumentalist and songwriter, Josh's music is celebrated and integrated into the repertoire of congregations, camps and communities around the world. Josh's music bridges themes of Jewish identity and continuity with razor-sharp lyricism and a progressive, radio-ready sound. With a high-energy and captivating performance style, Josh consistently brings strong feelings of uplift and community to audiences and congregations alike. Delivering high-octane Jewish rock, the Josh Nelson Project is five of the most talented performers in the United States. Touring the United States and abroad, the band is a perfect choice for community concerts, inspiring Shabbat services, and artist residencies.

DAN NICHOLS is one of the most popular and influential Jewish musicians in North America, performing over 200 concerts a year. His music has become an important part of the Reform Jewish movement, with synagogue youth and clergy alike incorporating it into their curriculum and services. His last two albums have garnered critical acclaim and a legion of growing fans. Songs like "L'takein (The Na Na Song)," "B'tzelem Elohim," "Kehilah Kedoshah," and "My Heart is in the East" are some of the most popular songs in Reform Judaism today.

MIKEY PAUKER is a Jewish/folk/soul recording artist hailing out of Los Angeles, California. Mikey grew up nestled in the hills of Laguna in South Orange County. He has received critical acclaim for his release of *Sim Shalom*, a collection of progressive Jewish songs that demands us to celebrate our differences, accept change and love each other. Mikey Pauker teaches communication and spirituality through Jewish music, as an artist-in-residence and song leader for hire in child, young adult, adult and family Jewish education. Mikey has had the ability to share the stage with Dan Nichols and E18hteen, Craig Taubman, Moshav, Kosha Dillz, Jeff Klepper, and Rick Recht, among others.

JAY RAPOPORT rocks out religious school! Taking the values and stories of the Jewish people, he transforms them into "Ruach Rock", a catchy piano-pounding style influenced by Billy Joel and Ben Folds. Jay's first album of original Jewish songs, *With All Your Heart*, was released in November 2010 and sold more than 1,000 copies within its first few weeks of release. An award-winning songwriter, Jay has performed with Craig Taubman, Josh Nelson, and Naomi Less, and was featured as an "emerging artist" on Jewish Rock Radio. Known at the Hava Nashira songleading conference for his witty, written-on-the-spot songs, Jay is now touring synagogues with his unique blend of instant sing-alongs and engaging musical storytelling that gets people out of their seats and rocking! He honed his skills as a camp and religious school songleader, touring clubs and colleges up and down the East coast with various bands, and incorporating original music into his roles as Camp Director at Temple Rodef Shalom in Falls Church, Virginia and as Youth Advisor and Educator at Congregation Rodeph Sholom in New York City. Jay studied piano and vocal performance at Berklee College of Music, and received his Bachelor's degree in music and elementary education at The College of William & Mary. He is currently pursuing a Master's Degree in Religious Education at Hebrew Union College in New York City.

RICK RECHT is one of the top touring musicians in Jewish music, playing over 150 dates each year in the United States and abroad. Rick has revolutionized and elevated the genre of Jewish rock music as a powerful and effective tool for developing Jewish pride and identity in youth and adults across the country. Rick is the national music spokesman for the Jewish National Fund and is the Executive Director of Songleader

Boot Camp, a national song leader training immersion program held annually in St. Louis. Rick is also the founder of Judaism Alive, a non-profit organization spearheading the launch of Jewish Rock Radio, the very first high-caliber international Jewish rock internet radio station. Rick has played at literally hundreds of URJ, Ramah, JCC, and private camps around the country as well as having been featured in concert and as scholar-in-residence at the NFTY, BBYO, and USY International Conventions, the URJ Biennial, the American Conference of Cantors, the Central Conference of American Rabbis, and Jewish communities across the United States. Rick has nine top selling Jewish albums.

PERI SMILOW uses music to make the world better. As an international performing artist, composer, educator and activist, she uses her talent, passion, and commitment to community to create social change through the arts. Peri's music and message of *tikkun olam* have been heard throughout the United States, Canada, England, Singapore and Israel. Peri has released four albums, including *Songs of Peace*, *Ashrey* and *The Freedom Music Project: The Music of Passover and the Civil Rights Movement* featuring an electrifying, 18-voice choir of young black and Jewish singers. Peri's newest release, *Blessings*, draws on her experience as a cancer survivor, wife and mother, and celebrates the importance of her relationships with loved ones, friends, community and faith. *Blessings* was co-produced by Grammy award winner Ben Wisch, and features the *Ruach 5771* selection "Hineini". Peri's favorite role is being mom to daughter Allie.

Formed in 2007, **SOULAVIV** is a four-person vocal group from Santa Barbara, CA, and in three short years has performed around the world at synagogues, JCCs, conferences, college campuses, and Jewish festivals. Singing in English and Hebrew, their music is infused with the sounds of folk, Motown, gospel, Memphis soul, and the great harmony groups of the 60's and 70's. Socially conscious lyrics mixed with Jewish heritage, spirituality, and celebration, plus a little California sunshine thrown in, make SoulAviv a unique musical experience they think you're really going to like. At the recent 2010 International Jewish Music Competition in Amsterdam, Netherlands, SoulAviv made it all the way to the Top 12, and were the highest placed band from the United States. SoulAviv is Jamie Green, Liat Wasserman, Rob Raede, and Roxanne Morganstern.

CRAIG TAUBMAN's dynamic music and moving performance style have been an inspiration to the Jewish community for almost 30 years. His passion for communal prayer is reflected in his CD projects, including the revolutionary *Friday Night Live*, *One Shabbat Morning*, and his newest release, *How Good*. Craig is also devoted to creating soundtracks for Jewish life via his *Celebrate* Series of music, featuring hundreds of artists from all walks of life. Craig enjoys a successful career in television and film, composing music for Fox, Showtime, HBO, PBS, New Line Cinema, Paramount and Disney.

CANTOR NATALIE YOUNG was invested in 2006 by Hebrew Union College-Jewish Institute of Religion in New York City and is already emerging as an original voice in Jewish music. In addition to working as an accomplished and talented vocalist, guitarist, and pianist, Cantor Young has composed more than fifty original liturgical and secular works, many of which are being used by communities around the country. Her debut solo album, *Carry Me*, gained great recognition when it was released in 2006. Her talents as a singer and songwriter have brought her to perform both across the country from Shreveport, Louisiana to Fairbanks, Alaska, and internationally in places such as Israel, Canada, and Russia. She is currently serving as the cantor at Ramat Shalom in Plantation, Florida. She is a member of the American Conference of Cantors, and is the recipient of numerous awards, including the 2004 Dr. Joseph Memorial Prize for Excellence in Composition and the 2005 Guild of Temple Musicians Award. She and her husband, Rabbi David Young, have two sons, Gabriel and Alexander and a daughter Isabella.